Table Of Contents

Chapter 1:   The Highway of Passion

Chapter 2:   Finding Your True Passion

Chapter 3:   Reviving Passion

Chapter 4:   Passion Force 1 - Curiosity

Chapter 5:   Passion Force 2 - Challenge

Chapter 6:   Passion Force 3 - Legacy

Chapter 7:   Passion Force 4 - Faith

Chapter 8:   Passion Force 5 – Altruism

Chapter 9:   Passion Force 6 - Epiphany

Chapter 10:   Passion at Home

Introduction

You cannot become rich or achieve any other kind of success in life if you don't have passion about what you are doing. Be it the simplest thing or the most sophisticated thing, you need passion in order to succeed.

Here we take a look at how important passion is and what different forms it must take in order to point our lives in the right direction, i.e. in the direction of super success.

Chapter 1: The Highway of Passion

What's the importance of passion in your life? Where does it take you?

The Highway of Passion

"When work, commitment, and pleasure all become one and you reach that deep well where passion lives, nothing is impossible."

You have a 9 to 5 job drawing a good pay, you have a good family and all's well with the world. But deep inside, you feel like you are going nowhere. The job isn't moving upward either. You are actually stagnating in your career and mentally and spiritually. Something is missing.

Passion. The one quality that textbooks and instruction manuals and company procedures will never talk about. Everyone is in such a hurry to make you fit perfectly into the machine like a well-oiled gear, that they forgot you are a living, feeling human being. Even you have forgotten.

Ask yourself. If I had a million bucks in the bank, what kind of work would I be doing? Would I chuck this humdrum job and move on to something really exciting? Something that I have always wanted to do? Then ask yourself – why am I not doing that right now? Is it because of peer pressure or because I don't want to move out of my comfort zone? Don't want to rock my boat? You are half asleep in your boat already and in a few years; you could be put out to pasture! If the boat rocks now, you could be jerked awake and come to your senses. Your passionate senses.

In the aftermath of the recession of 2008, millions of people lost their jobs. Many of them took up new vocations and suddenly found that they were finally following their dream. Many of them are now highly successful in their newfound professions.

You don't have to wait for dire straits to rock you out of your present mediocre life. You can decide right now, that you want to live and work passionately and make your life worthwhile. The Highway of Passion is an amazing ride. And Prosperity is just one of the landmarks on this route! Get ready for the ride of your life!

Chapter 2: Finding Your True Passion

What's your real calling in life?

Finding Your True Passion

"Nothing great in the world has been accomplished without passion.'

– Georg Hegel, German philosopher

So you have decided to break away from the pathetic monotony of your regular job. You want to live fully and passionately and reap all those rich rewards at the end of the rainbow. How do you find out what you are truly passionate about?

How do you separate the delusions from the do-able? You could be passionate about becoming the King of Spain, or winning the lottery or ruling the world. Indeed, there are people who have dreamt of that and done it. Alexander the Great ruled almost the entire known world in his time. But what is your true passion?

Here are a few steps you can take to discover the currents that move you deep inside: -

1. Read your own body language. How does your body behave at your present job? Does it tense up and ache all the time? Do you get panic attacks very often? Are you so bored that you doze at your desk? Do you keep looking at the clock as break time approaches? Then you are in the wrong job. You simply don't have the passion for it. When you work on a job that you are passionate about, all your aches and cramps will dissolve. You will find yourself working extra hours,

talking to your friends about your work and simply bubbling with life.

2. What did you love doing as a child? Your childhood hobbies and obsessions can indicate a genuine passion. Education and family pressures often move us away from our true calling. Did you love bikes or gardening or trekking? Then maybe a career in the automobile or landscaping or travel industries is where you should be! So sit back and recall your childhood and write down your memories. What made you smile then may still make you grin today and in the future.

3. What do you love doing as an adult? You might very well have passionate side pursuits even today. Do you love your moonlighting job more than your regular day job? Many corporate honchos work the night shift as chefs or night school teachers. Start spending a few hours every day on your pet hobby. It may just hold the key to the real you!

Chapter 3: Reviving Passion

Passion can be unleashed in various ways; one way is to change the circumstances that engulf you.

Reviving Passion

"Rest in reason; move in passion'

Sometimes to unleash true passion in yourself, you may have to change your job to suit your aptitude better. But you may find that you do love your existing job, but simply don't feel very passionate about it. You can study your situation and then try to make a few changes to rekindle the passion you felt when you first started working.

Visualize yourself working passionately at your job. What would you be feeling? A sharp focus, clear vision of your future, total control and mastery over your work, a healthy body and an exuberant attitude! Then reverse-engineer these symptoms to regain your passion.

Check on whether you work better with a team on the field rather than those solitary hours at a desk. Are you logical minded or creative minded? Are you crunching numbers when you would rather be in the design section? Get a revised aptitude assessment done. Ask your superior for a transfer to a more appropriate department.

Exercise your body for at least thirty minutes every day. Let the adrenalin pump and flow in your blood. Eat healthy food and drink a lot of water. Quit smoking and using any stimulants. Restore the balance between your spirituality and physicality by meditation and prayer. Your refreshed body will invigorate your mind and passion will return.

Increase your knowledge of your field by taking new study courses. Take time out to travel and widen your perspective. Take a half-pay sabbatical to add new qualifications to your resume. Some lateral career movement can bring an innovative twist in your way of working.

Passion does not come overnight. Taking these proactive steps will see a gradual increase in your enthusiasm. You will begin working with a newly fired zeal, which becomes contagious, motivating your teammates as well. You will have consciously taken charge of your life again and the fruits of prosperity will be in sight once again.

Chapter 4: Passion Force 1 - Curiosity

Curiosity is one igniter of true passion.

Passion Force 1 - Curiosity

What drives passionate people to work so hard? Where do they get their energy? Passion can be fueled by many factors. Let us examine 6 most important sources of the Force.

Curiosity. One of the most powerful triggers of human invention has been curiosity. Why does something happen? How does lightning occur? What happens if you mix two chemicals? Which route will discover new lands? The human mind is programmed to question everything around it.

Discoveries take place when this curiosity becomes a passionate driving force. It takes on a relentless unstoppable energy, which will not rest until a solution is found. Thomas Alva Edison tried out thousands of versions of the electric light bulb until he came up with one that worked. Madame Curie and her husband Pierre Curie spent all their lives unlocking the secrets of radioactivity. Steve Jobs' search for a better computer user interface finally gave us the Apple computer with the now familiar graphical user interface using icons, which eventually spread to the whole world of computing in the form of Microsoft's Windows.

Christopher Columbus, Vasco da Gama, Roald Amundsen and all the great explorers of the world travelled passionately in the quest of conquering new land for humanity. After centuries of looking up at the moon, Neil Armstrong and Edwin Aldrin actually walked on the lunar surface. Nothing can stop the force of curiosity and the determination that it fires up.

Success stories in the workplace often arise out of sheer

ignorance. An employee may find he knows nothing about a particular field and begins learning it to satisfy his own curiosity. Pretty soon he has mastered it and is teaching the world a few new things about it.

So step out of your 'known zone' and venture into the unknown. There just may be a discovery waiting there, with your name written on it.

Chapter 5: Passion Force 2 - Challenge

Without challenge in your life, you could hardly make the most of what you are passionate about. Infuse your passion with the right quest and you will do much better at it.

Passion Force 2 - Challenge

Our search for the sources of passion brings us to yet powerful factor – Challenge.

A challenge can be posed by a person upon himself or by external forces. A personal challenge can arise from adverse circumstances of poverty or deprivation. Rags-to-riches stories have been told for hundreds of years now. Even Presidents of countries have arisen from humble beginnings and risen to their positions of power by the sheer force of their passion.

Family prestige and a desire to prove one's mettle to one's elders and t society can also act as a challenging force. When a son inherits a business built by his father, he is propelled to expand that enterprise and thus demonstrate his own prowess. While most companies have boards of directors and public equity, in many traditional societies, it is the family-driven businesses that persevere, even over the centuries.

Targets set by corporate leadership also act as challenged to work teams. A keen competitive spirit between rival groups can set off a passionate chase of the markets. Pepsi and Coca Cola, Nike and Adidas, are a couple of examples of passionate rivalry, with each seeking to outdo each other in the pursuit of a better product and more sales. In these mega rivalries, passionate employees move quickly up the corporate ladder. Belief in the company's goals and ideals is essential to engender passion in employees.

Sometimes the source of the challenge may lie closer to home. The love of a woman or one's children can drive a man to succeed with the intent of providing better care and education for them. We are motivated to buy a larger and better house, a bigger and faster car, the latest cell phones and clothes. All these must- haves also act as challenges and rewards for our work.

It is up to each individual to determine what challenges him or her and then as Nike's motto says – Just do it! Your natural challenge instinct will push you through. When a mountaineer was asked why he climbed a mountain, he answered – Because it is there! Its very existence as an insurmountable peak was a challenge to him!

Chapter 6: Passion Force 3 - Legacy

When tapping on your passion, one thing that should be uppermost in your mind is that you need to leave a legacy for others.

Passion Force 3 - Legacy

When you are young, your motivation for working and living lies in larger income, better standards of living and in general having a good time. But as you grow older, your priorities change. You want something more fulfilling. You seek to achieve goals that you will be remembered for. A sense of urgency begins to set in as time passes. And the source of your passion arises from wanting to leave behind a legacy.

That legacy may take the form of social change brought about by your work. Or it can be in an enterprise or institution founded by you. Many successful businessmen set up foundations and trusts in the pursuit of noble causes. Thus they seek to perpetuate their name or family name for posterity. An invention or a new process or a novel product can also enshrine the maker's name in the books of history.

Temporal pleasures and petty rewards do not satisfy someone working at this level. His or her passion seeks loftier goals. The greater the goal, the more fervent the passion. Revolutionaries and freedom fighters like Mahatma Gandhi and Che Guevara struggled all their lives for the liberation of their countries. Their ambitions encompassed the lives of millions of their countrymen. The sheer magnitude of their legacy consumed their entire lifetime, but it was a passionate lifetime, with every day spent in pursuit of that goal.

How do you set about leaving behind your legacy? What is it

that you feel strongly about? Write down your strongest emotions and issues. They may even lie outside your present work area. Start working on those issues. Educate yourself and acquire new skills if you have to, and get to work. It may be a simple project like improving your community, or a major reform of state laws. Remember that all the great men and women who have brought about change were ordinary men like you and me, but they had the power of conviction and passionate belief in their dreams.

Chapter 7: Passion Force 4 - Faith

Be trusting. Have faith that you can realize the full potential of what you are passionate about.

Passion Force 4 – Faith

One of the most powerful engines of passion is faith in an external agency. Though faith may seem to have been marginalized in today's seemingly rational society, it still works behind the scenes in many areas.

Religion plays a dominant role in the lives of millions of people in the world today. Priests, nuns, monks, sadhus and mullahs are known to accomplish tremendous feats of social work and penance. Their faith in God and their religious ideals is the rocket fuel in their lives.

The term evangelical fervor come from a passion driven by a belief in God and the desire to convert other people to your way of thinking. This passion has sent explorers out to new lands, triggered numerous holy wars and changed entire demographics and cultures.

Oriental martial artists go through harsh training regimens and become lean mean human fighting machines. Their ruthless discipline arises from the strict codes of their specific martial art. Their devotion to this credo and their all-consuming faith in the mentor or sensei turns their lives into passionate experiences, which are not for the feeble or faint of heart.

In modern sports we see the same phenomenon displayed with players and their coaches. A dynamic coach can inspire his team to put in a passionate performance. If the players do not have faith in the coach or their fellow teammates, the team fails to coordinate and the game is lost. The faith equation between sportsman and trainer is particularly important in endurance sports like gymnastics and athletics.

A footballer may in turn be driven by his faith in his fans. A corporate executive may be passionate about his employees and shareholders. Faith, emotion and inspiration are alive and kicking in every corner of human activity.

Which external agency are you focusing on? God? Your boss? Your coach? Your community or country? Decide on what moves you and use that agency as a star to guide you and drive your passion.

Chapter 8: Passion Force 5 - Altruism

Blend your passion with the thought of doing good to humankind.

Passion Force 5 - Altruism

Altruism is defined as 'unselfish regard for or devotion to the welfare of others' and also 'behavior by an animal that is not beneficial to or may be harmful to itself but that benefits others of its species'. How does altruism become a force of passion? In the ongoing recession we have seem millions of jobs being lost. Many of these people have taken up volunteer work in social or environmental organizations. And quite a number of them have discovered that this selfless work gives them more satisfaction than their high paying job ever gave them. Their paradigm has shifted from the prosperity of the body to the prosperity of the soul.

The concept of altruistic work has often been mocked by an aggressive materialistic society. Social workers are called 'do-gooders' and there is always a cynical and contemptuous ring to that phrase. But after years of ruthless ladder climbing, people often cherish the ability to be themselves and help other people. Bill Gates of Microsoft built a huge empire through ruthless corporate tactics, often getting embroiled in monopolistic practice lawsuits. But after all that, he set up an equally huge foundation that disburses vast sums of money to fight disease and improve education.

Altruism is generally overruled by stronger passions geared towards material success in the early years, but as age advances, altruistic thoughts resurface and become a primary passion in most of us. This is probably because we know that great people are remembered less for the millions that they make, but rather for their service to humanity.

No volunteer or social worker ever starved. While there aren't any millions to make in selfless service to the lesser-privileged sections of humanity, the rewards of spiritual fulfillment are tremendous. The same passion that runs a corporate unit can be brought into play in running a successful Non-Governmental Organization or a Not for Profit outfit. All your skills can be well utilized in these noble ventures and you will see your passion suddenly multiply.

Chapter 9: Passion Force 6 – Epiphany

Understand everything you need to know about your passion. You never know when you achieve your nirvana.

Passion Force 6 – Epiphany

One of the definitions of epiphany is 'A comprehension or perception of reality by means of a sudden intuitive realization.' That's a moment in your life when you are suddenly struck by a powerful thought that changes your life forever.

A lifelong passion can be triggered by an epiphany. Saul the persecutor of the followers of Jesus Christ undergoes an epiphany on the road to Damascus and his life is changed forever. He went on to becoming one of Christ's greatest apostles.

Such a life changing incident occurs in the lives of many great men. It may be something provocative that someone says to you. It may be the sight of another human being suffering. It can be a sudden realization that you hate your present job and you decide what you really want to do in life. Sometimes an epiphany can be a harsh tragic event like the demise of a family member or some colossal disaster somewhere in the world. Your eyes open wide and all the shades fall off. You can see clearly around you and far ahead.

You do not have to sit and await an epiphany to change your life. Read good works of literature, listen to inspiring music and songs, travel around, meet people and you will be struck by a light on your own road to Damascus.

The Epiphany is also a Christian feast that celebrates God being revealed to Man in the form of Jesus Christ. So this can be taken as a metaphor for the spiritual being in us manifested in the physical form. Which is what passion is all about. Our spiritual energy driving our material body to achieve ideals and goals that are godlike!

Inventors and discoverers experience epiphanies all the time. Archimedes was struck by his discovery of buoyancy and ran out yelling – Eureka! Eureka!

May you too experience an epiphanic moment and share old Archie's happiness!

Chapter 10: Passion at Home

You needn't go much far to realize your passion.

Passion at Home

Getting passionate about your career and blazing a glorious path at the office is great. But don't let your loved ones suffer from a lack of passion at home. A proper balance has to be struck by giving love to your spouse and children too.

A passionate lifelong affair with your wife or husband can do wonders in your work life too. You are happy and relaxed and your body glows with the healing effects of healthy loving sex. The love you shower on your children is also reciprocated many times over.

A man is truly respected if he excels in all his roles – as a worker, a son, a husband and a father (and even a grandfather) and a community member. Devote time and passion to all these roles. When you have genuinely mastered the art of passion, you will find that it pervades every minute of your day, be it in the boardroom or bedroom or playroom.

Passion can become a double-edged sword if not wielded properly. Spending hours and hours of obsessed extra time at the workplace can affect your health as well as your family relations. Neglecting to attend your son's school events and not cheering him at his football match can create an alienation that can never be repaired. An unfulfilled spouse can also prove very damaging in the long run. A marriage can fall apart and a string of unhappy one-night stands can never take the place of a loving caring relationship.

Passion is not about throwing huge family parties where everyone can feed on your wealth. It isn't about giving a no-limit credit card to your wife or the latest bike to your son. It is spending time and effort to share your life and soul with your loved ones. Passion lies in transmitting your passion for life to your children, your wife and all around you.

Conclusion

Your passion could be a great tool that could take you places. Don't stifle it. Don't let it die.

Instead, give it the right fuel and watch it blaze like an inferno. This would be the inferno of your success.

The End

www.ingramcontent.com/pod-product-compliance
Lightning Source LLC
Chambersburg PA
CBHW081823170526
45167CB00008B/3522